simple
wire & metal
style

simple

wire & metal

style

DEBORAH SCHNEEBELI MORRELL

Photographs by Heini Schneebeli

WATSON-GUPTILL PUBLICATIONS/NEW YORK

Acknowledgements

Very special thanks to Heini Schneebeli for his care and attention to detail in taking the
photographs in this book. My gratitude extends to all the unknown artists and artisans
whose work constantly serves as an inspiration to me.

For my Godchildren
Louis Arthur Lloyd Pack
and
Beatrice Antonia Minns

✤

First published in the United States in 1998
by Watson-Guptill Publications,
a division of BPI Communications, Inc.
1515 Broadway, New York, NY 10036

Library of Congress Catalog Card Number: 98-60301

ISBN: 0-8230-4808-X

1 2 3 4 5 6 7 8 9/06 05 04 03 02 01 00 99 98

Published by MQ Publications, Ltd.
254-258 Goswell Road, London EC1V 7EB

Copyright © MQ Publications, Ltd. 1998

Text © Sacha Cohen 1998
Photographs © Lucinda Symons 1998
Stylist Diana Civil

Series Editor: Ljiljana Ortolja-Baird
Editor: Jane Warren
Designer: Bet Ayer

Printed in Italy

contents

✣

introduction

❖

Metal and wirework are currently enjoying a resurgence of interest. For those who might be interested, working with metal and wire is not difficult or beyond the normal range of craft skills. In my attempt to demystify these crafts and to make them accessible to more people, I have created a range of creative and unusual projects to either decorate the home or to make as gifts. Each project incorporates simple, traditional skills and a range of materials and tools that are available in your local shopping or garden centers. In fact, many tools are common household objects and you will only need to spend money on expensive equipment when you make the transition from beginner to experienced craftsperson. Many projects are small enough to be made in an evening and do not require special equipment, time consuming preparation or expensive materials. For me, it is this challenge of designing and creating a beautiful project from something so simple and ordinary as a piece of wire or a square of foil which excites my imagination.

Wire

So many types of wire are available, all with different qualities and degrees of pliablility, and it is this infinite adaptability that has made it so appealing to craftspeople and artists for centuries. Jewelers and sculptors in particular have exploited the potential of the medium using techniques such as weaving, welding, knotting, molding, knitting and sewing.

The technique for wire production goes back almost a thousand years, when it was a laborious and intensive hand process. Long before mechanization, which arrived in England in the mid-sixteenth century, drawing machines were invented and the metal was drawn through holes in a heavy metal draw plate. The iron used at that time corroded quickly and it wasn't until the nineteenth century that wire was commercially treated by coating it with tin to prevent rust from occurring.

During the Victorian era, Britain and France had thriving wire industries which manufactured many functional and decorative items, from elegant, intricately woven garden furniture to more humble domestic implements. Many examples of wirework dating from this time can still be seen today and are appealing to collectors. It was only with the invention and mass-production of cheaper plastic products that the demise of wire-based products began.

INTRODUCTION

Some cultures today, notably in third world countries such as Zimbabwe and Zambia, produce the most extraordinarily inventive sculptures using recycled wire, often faithfully reproducing shapes with amazing proportional accuracy. The Masai are famed for weaving brightly colored baskets from old telephone cables. It is not difficult to see why this versatile medium has appeal for artists and craftspeople. American artist Alexander Calder, creator of simple, striking wire sculptures has proved inspirational and his work was the influence for the ring hand project on page 20.

Metal

Like wirework, the art of working with thin sheet metal has a long history, and some outstanding early examples of the craft still exist today. Trade or shop signs, now made from plastic, were once fashioned in metal in the form of the merchandise sold, a boot or shoe for a shoemaker, and a hat for a milliner.

Metalwork craft traditions were imported to the New World from Europe by craftsmen settlers from the late sixteenth century onwards. When tin became widely available in the nineteenth century, a proliferation of practical and decorative objects followed. Weathervanes, pierced lanterns, candle sconces and pie safes are typical examples of what have now become highly prized examples of American folk art. Stunning examples of elaborate inn signs still exist on seventeenth-century central European buildings today. Mexico has a long-established tradition of tin ware. Historically most metalwork was devoted to religion in the form of altar pieces, candlesticks and highly decorated frames for sacred icons. Today, Mexico remains one of the most successful producers of metal crafts for the interior decor and gift trade in Europe and America. The techniques used are simple – like those employed in the projects in the book – cutting, stamping, piercing, scoring and embossing. Other cultures produce fantastic items using recycled metal – a suitcase from Africa made with woven strips of steel cans or a well-designed jug made from colorfully printed oil cans in India. Aluminum, copper or brass would not have been available to these talented folk artists as it was and still is far too expensive to use. Today recycled metal is relatively inexpensive and easily obtainable.

The skills and techniques involved in producing a wire or metal project may appear intricate and complicated on first sight, since for most of us these are unfamiliar materials to work with. While it is true that "practice makes perfect," special skills are not required, only the imagination to carry your ideas through. My range of projects is simple enough for a beginner to attempt and allows plenty of scope for adapting as your enthusiasm for these versatile media increases.

working with wire

▶ 11

W ire is a truly versatile medium. Its appeal for me is in the challenge of creating something sophisticated and stylish and above all useful from a material that is plain and nondescript in its manufactured form. Twisted, coiled, braided, looped, bound and beaded, wire can be manipulated into a myriad of shapes using only the aid of basic everyday tools. Improve its strength by twisting strands together and at the same time, twist in a second color to add another dimension to your project. Like metal foil, wire is pliable and extremely durable. It is available in a huge variety of gauges (thicknesses) and metal types. Each varies in thickness, temper and color.

Most people are familiar with green plastic-coated gardening wire. It is available in different gauges and the thicker wires are extremely springy, but very easy to manipulate. Its plastic coating makes it particularly suited to outdoor use. Galvanized wire is commonly available in five different gauges. It is made of steel and coated with zinc to prevent it from corroding and is suitable for outdoor use. Its sturdy properties make it suitable as a strong base for projects which are used as containers.

Soft copper wire has a pink tinge making it particularly appealing for decorative projects. Tinned copper wire is stronger than ordinary copper wire and does not tarnish when handled. Brass picture wire is available in short rolls. It is extremely strong since it is made of a number of strands twisted together.

Wire is widely available, relatively cheap to purchase and available in a huge variety of gauges and metal types. All types of wire are suitable for twisting – a technique which produces a decorative, strong and flexible wire. All wire types are available from specialty craft stores, while more common, multipurpose wires are commonly found in garden centers and hardware stores.

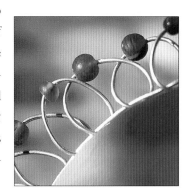

WORKING WITH WIRE

t w i s t e d   w i r e
e g g   s p o o n

✣

This simple project is a perfect example of the decorative form of the spoon. Twisted galvanized wire can be formed easily into even and symmetrical shapes because the twisting technique produces tension in the wire, making it unlikely to kink. Using one length of wire, the bowl of the spoon is made from wire manipulated into loops, while the handle is formed into a traditional heart.

These decorative projects have a practical function too – you really will be able to toast a piece of bread on an open fire and lift an egg safely out of a pan of boiling water.

Detail of the looped wire manipulated into the bowl of the spoon.

Detail of the twisted wire fork.

plant
support

❖

Antique examples of twisted wire planters and furniture are highly sought after. The method of constructing these frames has barely changed. Nowadays, with the development of plastic coated wire, plant structures are longer lasting and are not subject to rust – an advantage if you enjoy working without gloves.

It would be impossible to buy such a pretty and practical plant support for the small cost of making it yourself. These frames are quickly and simply made from twisted thick green garden wire. The technique of twisting adds strength and flexibility. Once you have mastered the technique, the next step is to design your own.

The plant support is sturdy enough to support most plants.

aluminum mesh basket

❖

Stretched, tucked, pleated or molded, aluminum mesh is extremely soft, pliable and easy to work with. Obtained from an art or sculptor's supply store or hardware store, it is surprisingly similar to working with fabric, but without the inconvenience of fraying!

The body of the basket is molded over an upturned bowl and the excess mesh is pleated into shape. The handle, with scroll decoration, is bound to the basket base with fine wire.

Filled with chocolate candies or goodies for any holiday, the basket makes a stunning little gift.

This decorative basket is an example of just how attractive wire and mesh can be made to appear.

hand ring
holder

❖

Soft aluminum wire is very pliable and although it is relatively thick, it is easy to bend into smooth curves. Contemporary in appearance, this is an easy choice for a beginner, since the skills required are minimal. The challenge is in manipulating the shape from just one continuous length of wire. The form of the hand is a logical choice for a ring holder, but also ideal for hanging earrings from or draping necklaces over.

A simple template is provided, but as your confidence grows and you become adept at working with wire, design and create your own shapes, such as the winged bird pictured on page 23.

Once you've mastered the ring hand, design and make your own shapes.

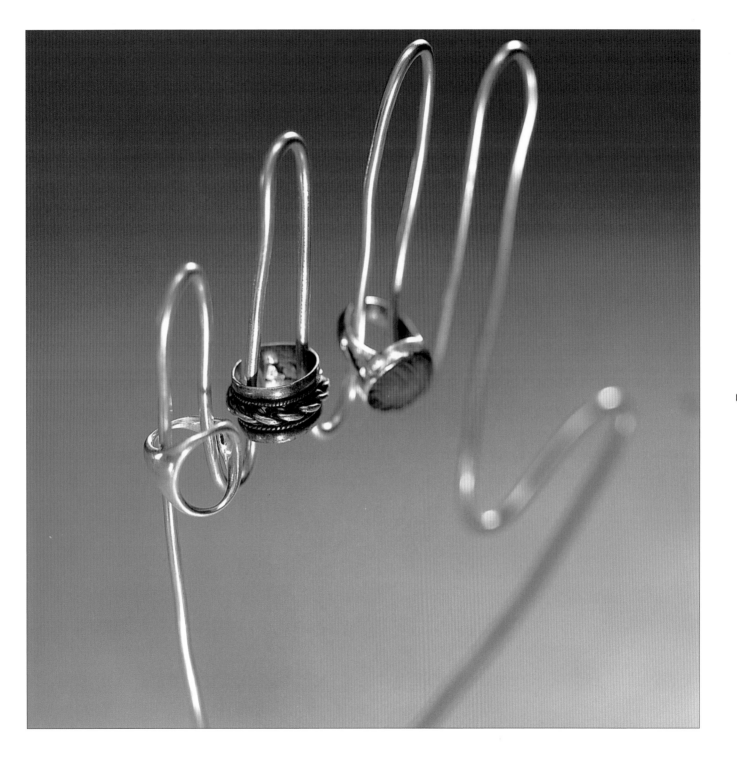

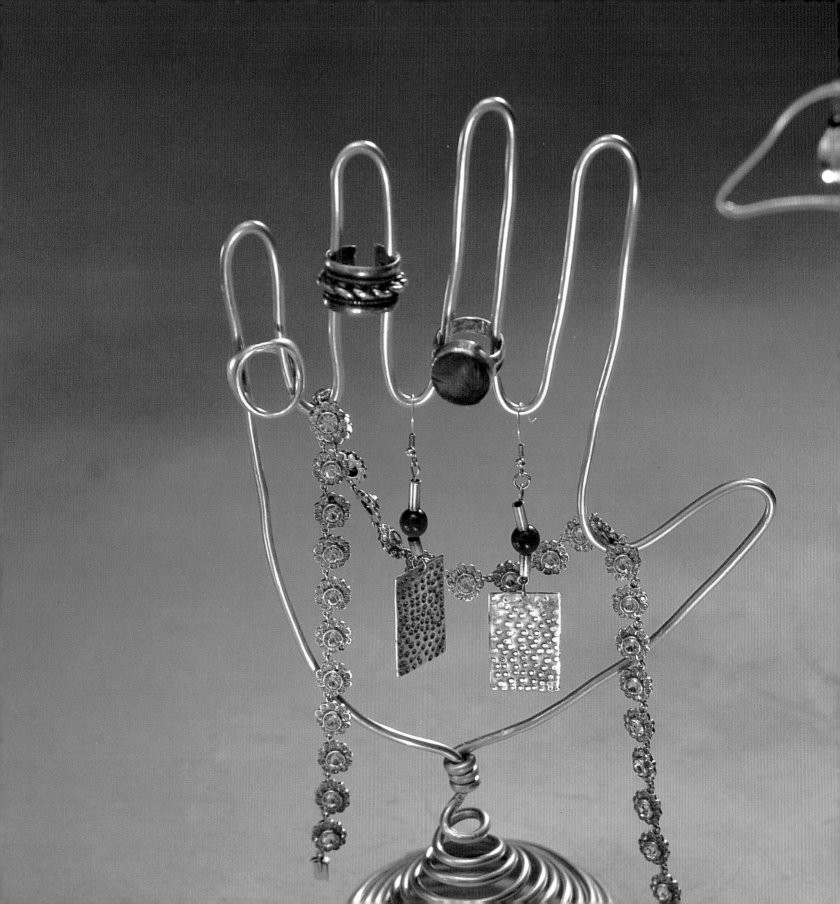

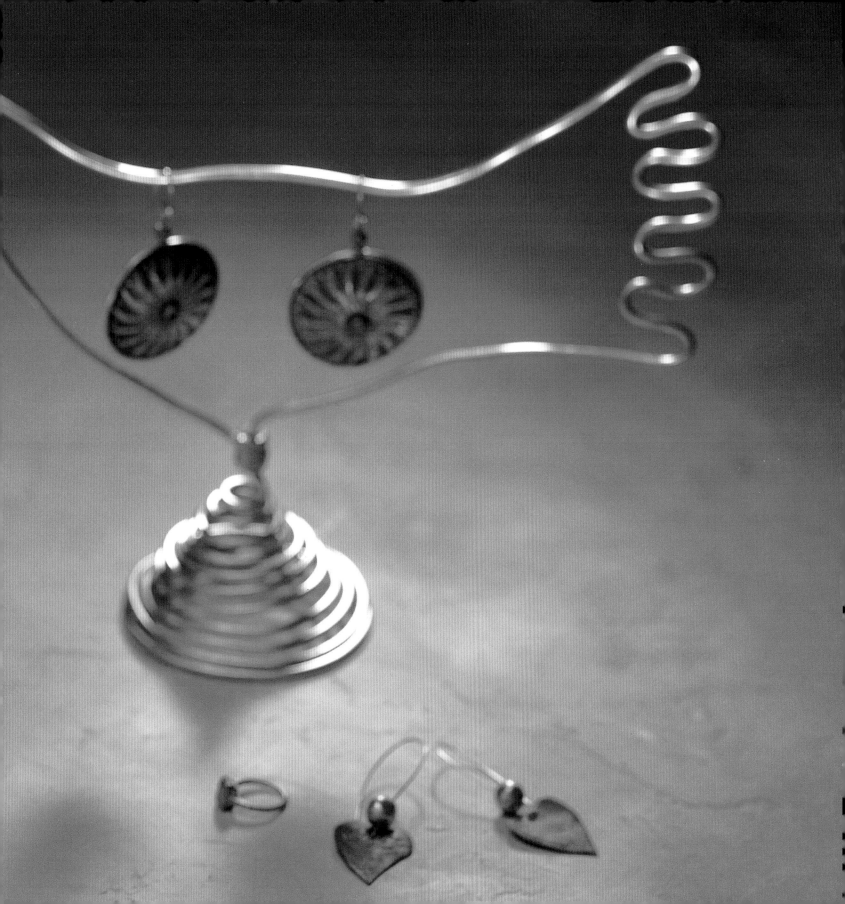

beaded
candle holder

❖

Take wirework techniques one stage farther and add a selection of your favorite or most unusual glass beads to create this exquisite candle holder. The wire frame is molded into the base of a tiny metal tart tin, the fluted sides holding the wire evenly in place. The whole of the design and construction of the piece is influenced by the shape and form of the tart tin. The basic shape can be adapted to a more complex or larger version once you've mastered the basic techniques.

When lit, the candle flame reflects in each facet of the colored glass beads, casting a subdued glittering light around the room.

folk art
egg basket

✛

This rustic little egg basket made from twisted soft copper wire has all the best qualities of folk art. Although the design is decorative, the pretty looped base acts as a practical stand to raise the basket from the ground making it easier to sit eggs in. The heart motif provides a perfect way to join two ends together. Apart from the base, all the wire used has been twisted, which gives it a decorative charm and makes it stronger so it will keeps its shape better. It is not complicated to make and, as with many of the other projects, requires only the use of wire cutters and pliers. The looped rim and base are made by wrapping the wire around a wooden spoon handle. Once you have made this project try adapting the technique to make other baskets in different shapes and sizes.

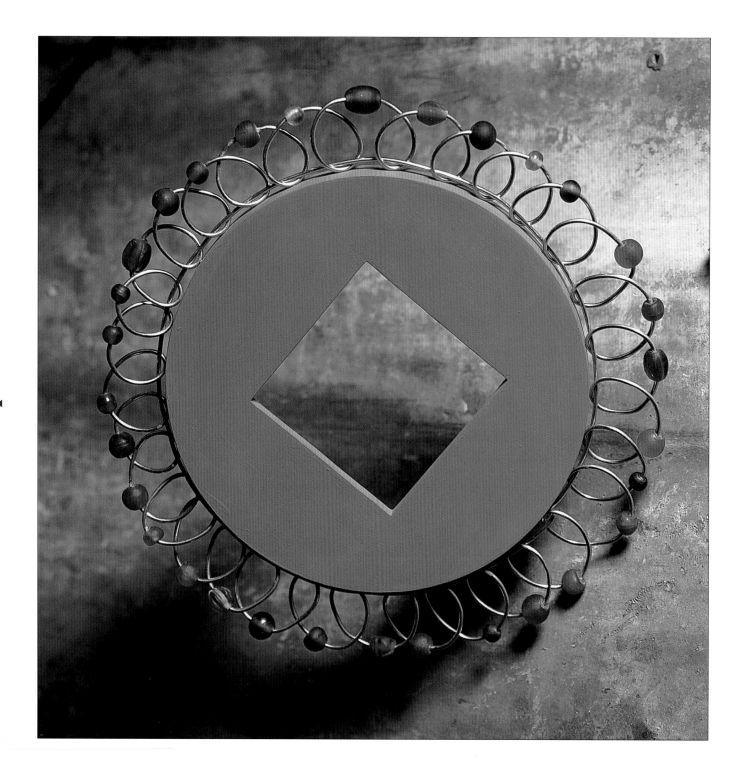

picture
frame

❖

A pair of pliers and some wire cutters are the only tools necessary to create this modern decorated frame. Aluminum or tinned copper wire are soft, so they can be twisted easily into looped circles. A number of irregularly shaped pretty blue and green glass beads have been threaded onto the silvery wire to off-set the deep blue of the painted round frame. The design lends itself to displaying a small mirror.

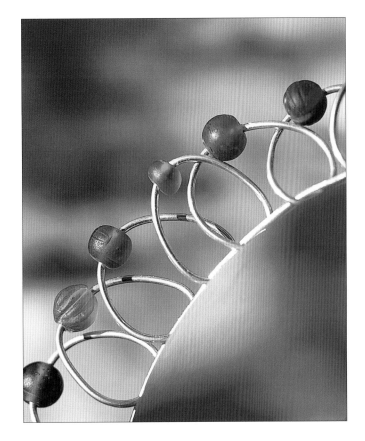

Alternate blue and green glass beads for best effect.

glass jar
lantern

✥

Find yourself a selection of attractively-shaped glass jars to make into votive candle holders. This is one of the simplest projects in the book, requiring few tools and materials or knowledge of complicated techniques. The galvanized wire is twisted tightly onto the rim of the jar, holding the handle securely in place.

Traditional outward-turned scrolls have been used to make the decorative join at the handle tops.

The lanterns have been designed for outside use and look effective arranged in a group or suspended from the branches of a tree.

Detail of the reversed heart-shape scrolls at the handle top.

christmas tree
decorations

❖

These simple candy-striped Christmas tree decorations incorporate wirework skills on a small scale. Create the candy stripe by twisting in a strand of pink anodized aluminum wire – discarded telephone or electrical wire are good alternatives.

The wire is bent into scrolls, a common decorative feature in wirework and bound together to form elegant pendant shapes. Translucent glass beads are suspended from the top of the ornament.

working with metal

▶ 35

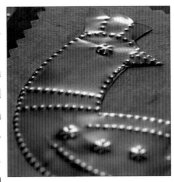

H ole-punched, embossed, folded, snipped, curled and indented – metal foil in all its forms is a versatile, durable and strong medium to work with. Brass, copper and aluminum each have their own unique properties and qualities. While some metal foils lend themselves to different projects, much depends on your personal preference. All are decorated in exactly the same way, but the harder, stronger metals require more pressure to make an

impression. Brass is the hardest coloring. Copper has a warm pink cut and decorate. Varnish any the color to tarnish with age. metal, light in weight and very tarnish. Metal foils and expanded obtainable in rolls 6in/15cm wide suppliers will cut to your required good home improvement stores,

metal and recognizable for its gold tinge. It is soft, pliable and easy to copper projects if you do not want Aluminum is a soft silvery-white malleable. It will not corrode or mesh or woven metal gauze are and 1yd/1m long, although some length. All are readily available from hardware stores and craft shops.

The metal foil most commonly used for the projects in this book is 0.1mm, although it is possible to make some projects in other gauges. All the foils are easy to cut with ordinary scissors, although care should always be taken. You will find working with metal foils very rewarding. The results are impressive and professional-looking and people find it hard to believe that they have been made by hand.

WORKING WITH METAL

cat face
bird scarer

❖

These prowling cats with their striking eyes are just the thing to scare away scavenging birds from the vegetable garden. Any gardener will tell you that crows in particular can be real pests pecking away at the corn in summer.

The eyes of the cat are made by gluing marbles into holes cut into the foil face. On bright sunny days they become almost luminous when the light shines through them. The effect is really quite realistic.

Use them decoratively by slotting the wire "stems" into the top of a garden cane and pushing the cane firmly into the soil.

metal foil
flowers

❖

Most people would never think of making flowers from metal but in reality, they are no more difficult to make than the paper version. The results are unusual, striking and enduring. These flowers were inspired by ornate flowery metal candlesticks found in many French churches. Extend the project and wire the flowers around a candlestick if you are feeling creative.

A tracing wheel has been used to create the pattern. The three-dimensional effect on the petals of the flower was accomplished by marking the lines alternately on the back and front of the cut-out flower.

A combination of all three metal foils has been used for this project – a good opportunity to learn of their different qualities first hand.

Foil flower with stamen-effect centers made of copper, aluminum and brass.

b r a s s
b u t t e r f l y

❖

Reminiscent of summer's colors with their delicate
and intricate markings, these shimmering golden
insects will liven up the greenhouse wall in winter.

Working with a design which has a symmetrical
shape is always satisfying and, since the butterfly
shape is decorative, the pattern used for the wing decoration can be less complicated. The three-dimensional effect is made by bending and molding the body
around a wooden spoon handle. For the finishing
touch, the antennae are wound around a thin knitting
needle to create the tight curls.

The unusual curved
three-dimensional body of the
butterfly is simply achieved by
bending the foil over a wooden
spoon handle.

42 ◀

44 ◀

house
candle shade

❖

This unusual candle holder is made from soft aluminum foil but it could be made from thicker aluminum. The design is inspired by Mexican punched tin light or lantern shades. The originals are well-known examples of Mexican tinwork, which is much admired. Tin is more difficult to cut and the edges need to be filed to remove dangerous rough edges.

The tracing wheel lines have punctured the metal allowing the candle light to shine through the tiny holes. The house is illuminated by two votive candles placed in glass jars for safety and thick, translucent tracing paper is fixed to the inside walls of the house to hide the candles.

Disguise bare candle flames with
these unusual candle holders.
Holes punctured in the surface
of the foil allows the light to
shine through.

crown
hook rack

❖

Simple shapes and symmetrical patterns always work well together. This project with its regal theme combines the most traditional wire and metalwork techniques. The embossed metal surface has been decorated using a tracing wheel. The wirework base is formed from thin twisted copper wire manipulated into the framework, and the hooks and infill detail are made using flattened coils and twisted wire.

For safety, hang below eye level and twist the hooks into an open circle to prevent them from catching clothes. The rack can be used in any room in the home – and would be particularly effective nailed inside near the front door as a rack for hanging keys on.

▶ 49

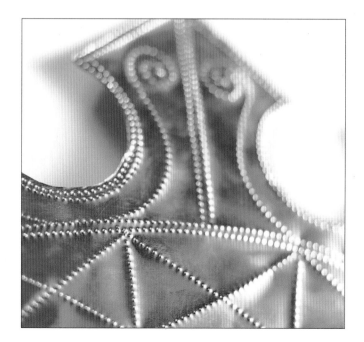

Detail of the embossed surface
of the foil crown.

brass gloved hand clasp

✣

Based on a common Victorian design, these elegant gloved hands are immensely decorative and useful. The brass is decorated using a tracing wheel and a dry ballpoint pen. Brass is a harder metal than aluminum or copper and so needs to be pressed harder to make the pattern clear. Its lovely glowing color is similar to gold and polishes beautifully using special metal polish.

The clasp part of the design is made by gluing a clothespin onto the back of the hand using rapid-setting epoxy. Use these glove clasps to hold all manner of things from stamps to decorative ribbons.

Detail of the raised decoration on the hand of the glove.

b i r d
g r e e t i n g
c a r d

✤

Stamped or embossed metal greeting cards are becoming widely available.

Copper foil is a warm-colored metal, soft enough to cut with scissors and easy to decorate by drawing and punching a design onto the back to produce a raised pattern on the front. The enduring quality of the metal means that the motif can be removed from the card and used for another decorative purpose, perhaps on the cover of a book, painted box or nailed to a cabinet door.

cheese
larder

❖

You don't need to search far in antique or junk shops to find an inexpensive old food cabinet which will lend itself to converting into a cheese larder. In the past, perforated zinc was commonly used as a screening mesh to keep out flies while American pie safes were traditionally made using punched tin.

Brass gauze or fine mesh is beautiful in combination with the warm gold effect of the brass foil decoration and complements the pale green cabinet frame. The embossed brass flowers and leaves and the braided brass wire stems are sewn onto the mesh using fine matching brass wire threaded through the fixing points. These are punched out using a hole punch.

Detail of the hole-punched fixing points on the flowers and leaves.

christmas
reindeer

✤

It takes minimal skill, tools and techniques to make this magical herd of sturdy Christmas reindeer. A backdrop of forest trees made from slightly thicker aluminum foil creates a wintry theme.

The instructions describe a simple system for making a three-dimensional object from a flat template. The raised pattern which catches and reflects the shimmering light is made by drawing on the back of the soft aluminum foil with a ballpoint pen.

This charming collection looks great on a Christmas mantelpiece or arranged under a simply decorated tree. Make them into a mobile by piercing the middle of the top of the back and threading them onto a 1.25mm (18 gauge) galvanized or aluminum wire frame.

WORKING WITH METAL

foil
wreath

❖

The soft yielding qualities of aluminum foil along with its silvery brilliance make it an ideal material to use to create this unusual wintry wreath. The "willow leaves" are cut freehand from the metal foil with a pair of scissors and the patterned leaf veins are surprisingly easily drawn using a dressmaker's tracing wheel. Although a little patience is required to attach the finished leaves to the wire frame, the end result of this simple project is quite stunning. The garland could be the focal point in a pale and minimally-decorated room. At a more festive time of year make it part of a restrained silver and white themed Christmas decor, perhaps setting the scene by displaying it on your front door.

Detail of the two different willow leaves.

plant name marker

❖

For those of us who plant a flower only to be unable to identify it months or years later because we've lost the name tag, these unusual plant markers are the perfect solution. The name will never wear away and the tag will not disintegrate.

The key shapes are cut from a roll of thin copper foil and the raised design is created by "drawing" on the back using a tracing wheel. The decorative stars are punched using a steel punch and a hammer (available from hardware or craft stores). To add a personal touch, use your own handwriting on the front of the marker to name the plant.

Copper is traditionally used for this purpose and its warm color complements the infinite palette of greens found among foliage in the house or garden. When left outdoors the copper will develop a typical verdigris patination – if you don't want this to happen just give the finished pieces a coat of varnish.

putting it together

materials

✜

1 **Copper foil** (0.1mm thick) – A warm pink metal; soft and very easy to cut and decorate.

2 **Copper strip** (0.2mm thick) – This slightly thicker copper is an alternative that can be used to make the plant name marker on page 63.

3 **Aluminum foil** (0.1mm thick) – A soft and pliable silver metal, easy to cut and decorate.

4 **Brass foil or shim** (0.1mm thick) – A gold-colored metal; hard and springy, it requires more pressure to decorate.

5 **Aluminum fine expanded mesh** – Extremely soft and pliable. It can be stretched, pleated, tucked, folded or molded around a solid form as well as cut with scissors.

6 **Woven brass gauze,** 20 holes per linear inch/eight per centimeter – Woven gauze is made by weaving together 0.3mm (30 gauge) brass wire. It can be manipulated in the same way as aluminum mesh, although it should be cut with strong scissors. Because brass is a relatively hard metal it is not suitable for molding.

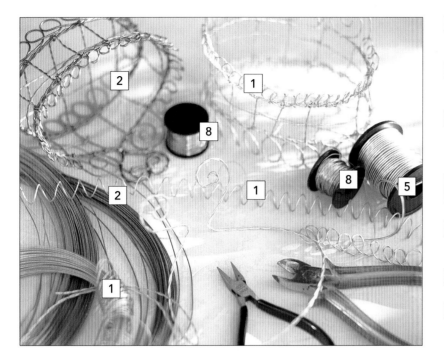

1 **Galvanized wire** – Silver, hard and springy; suitable for outdoor use; available in five different gauges (thicknesses).

2 **Soft copper wire** – Soft and pliable, very easy to use; a warm pink color which tarnishes with handling and exposure to air.

3 **Brass picture hanging wire** – Sold in small rolls 3yd/3m long at hardware stores; made from a number of strands of wire twisted loosely together; very strong.

4 **Aluminum wire** – Soft and easy to work with.

5 **Tinned copper wire** – Has a shiny finish, does not tarnish; harder than copper wire.

6 **Anodized aluminum wire** – Available in a wonderful array of colors; soft, pliable and easy to work with.

7 **Green gardening wire** – Suitable for outdoor use; easy to manipulate.

8 **Fine wires used for binding** – Available in brass, copper and tinned copper in 0.3mm (30 gauge).

The majority of the tools required for wire- and metalwork are familiar in many households. The following are commonly found in the household toolbox – wire cutters, pliers, hammer, drill, piece of dowel, and a small piece of wood.

Others will be found around the house – scissors, wooden spoon, knitting needle, ruler, blue tack, transparent and double-sided tape, tracing wheel (more commonly used in sewing), pinking shears, a knitting needle and an old phone book.

More specialized equipment includes a leather hole punch available from good tool shops; an awl for puncturing holes in foil and a steel punch with a motif on one end for stamping designs, available from more specialized art and sculptor's supply stores. A work bench with a vice is useful, quick setting epoxy is necessary for many projects and modeling tools are available from craft stores.

essential techniques

❖

Twisting wire

Twisting strands of wire together has many advantages: it looks decorative; it adds strength; and it increases flexibility, making it easier to create smooth spirals and curves.

It is easy to twist strands of soft or fine wire, such as copper, together using a hand-held drill. This method makes it possible to twist wire evenly and as loosely or tightly as the design requires. Harder or thicker wire such as the galvanized or green gardening wire are better twisted by hand using an implement such as a wooden spoon.

Twisting 2mm-thick (14 gauge) gardening wire

Cut a length of wire, approximately three times longer than the required twisted length. Bend the wire in half around a fixed point such as a stair banister and join the two ends by twisting them together in a counter-clockwise direction. Put the handle of a wooden spoon through the loop. Hold the handle in one hand and the spoon section in the other. Twist the wire in a clockwise direction. Pull the wire taut and keep it horizontal for an even twist. When the wire is twisted as tightly as is required, stop turning. Transfer your hold from the spoon to the wire and allow the spoon to unwind slightly and release the tension of the wire. Cut free with wire cutters.

Twisting 1mm (20 gauge) soft copper wire

Cut a length of wire approximately half a length longer than the required twisted length. Bend the wire as before, but this time feed the two cut ends into the chuck of a hand drill. Tighten to secure the ends. Keep the wire taut and turn the drill, twisting the wire to the required tension. Undo the chuck to release the wire. Cut the other end from the fixed point.

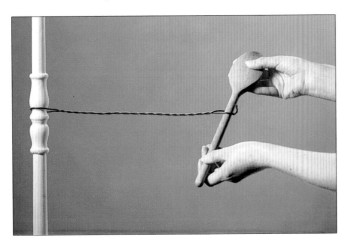

Gardening wire

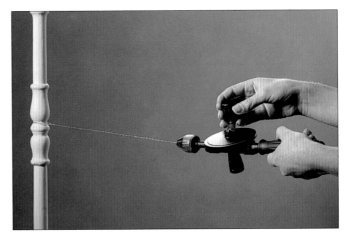

Copper wire

Twisting two colors together

Twist soft colored wire first, as instructed above. Bend thicker wire around the fixed point and twist all thicknesses together around a spoon handle in a counterclockwise direction. Work as for twisting thicker wire.

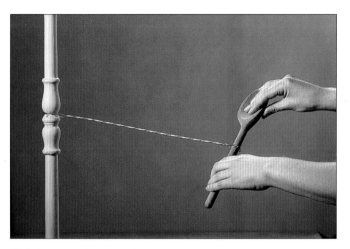

Twisting two colors together

Making spirals

Curl one end of the wire into a small loop, using pliers. Use your thumb to create an even tension to make a smooth curve.

Making spirals

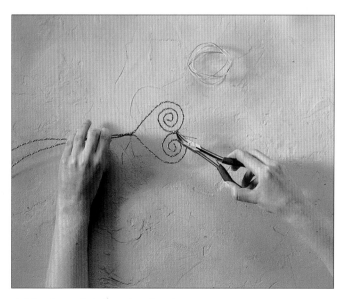

Judge the distance between the coils by eye

Joining two spirals to make a heart

Bend the straight section of the wire at 45° and bind three times with 1mm (20 gauge) galvanized wire. Bind the point where the spirals meet in the same way .

Joining two spirals to make a heart

Braiding brass picture wire

This is already stranded and twisted. Braiding makes it thicker and creates an unusual decorative material.

Fix a nail into the work surface. Tie three equal lengths of brass wire together and hook the knot around the nail. Braid evenly until you reach the required length.

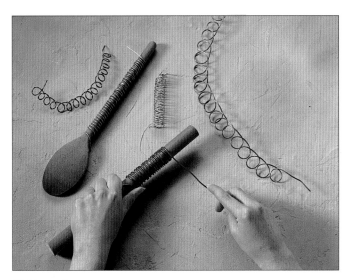

Making coils

Flattening coils

Remove the coil from the wood. Carefully and evenly flatten each loop by pressing each tightly between your fingers. Stretch the coil so that the individual loops are separate or allow them to overlap.

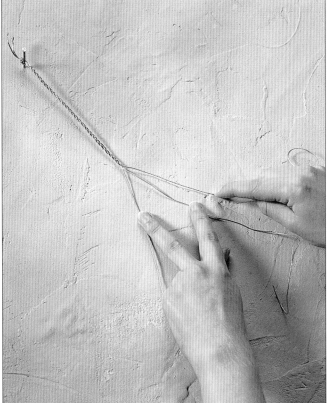

Braiding brass picture wire

Making coils

Coils are a useful decorative and structural feature commonly used in traditional wirework.

Wrap the wire tightly around a wooden spoon handle or dowel, depending on the size of coil required. Thicker wire requires greater manipulation.

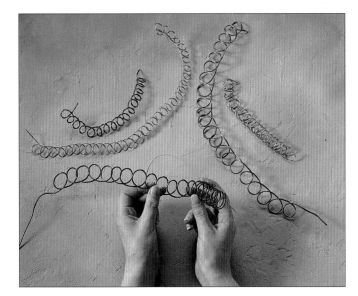

Flattening coils

Embossing aluminum foil

Aluminum is a soft pliable metal, easily marked with a dry ballpoint pen. Place the metal onto a yielding surface such as a phone book and "draw" the design by pressing very firmly. Drawing lines against a straight edge produces a quilted effect which appears as a raised surface on the other side.

Embossing aluminum foil

Copper punching

Use a ready made punch (available from an art or sculptor's supply store or good hardware store). Punch from the front to create an indented image. Punch from the back and the image will be a raised design on the front side. Place foil on a piece of wood. Position the patterned end of the punch and hit once firmly with a hammer.

Copper punching

Decorating brass using a tracing wheel

Place the metal on a telephone directory. Using the tracing wheel, press firmly to "draw" directly onto the metal. This is a quick and satisfying method of decorating metal foil – the pattern appears as a series of raised dots on the other side.

Decorating brass using a tracing wheel

twisted wire egg spoon

✤

Not just a decorative ornament, this twisted wire spoon is practical too!

MATERIALS
- *1.25mm-thick (18 gauge) twisted galvanized wire – 1²⁄₃yd/1.5m*
- *0.75mm-thick (22 gauge) galvanized wire – 4in/10cm*
- *Wire cutters*
- *Bent-nose pliers*

1 Beginning 15¾in/40cm from one end of the wire, make a series of six loops using approximately 12in/30cm in total.

2 Bring together the ends of the looped section to form a circle with the loops facing inwards. Hold the ends together with pliers and make four twists with your free hand.

3 Open the shaft of the handle and form an ellipse 5in/14cm long.

4 Bring the two wires together as before and make four more twists.

5 With pliers, form each wire end into a loose spiral using the same length of wire for each. Join them together so that the spirals touch at one side to make a symmetrical heart.

6 Bind the join four times with the second length of wire and twist the ends tightly together to secure. Trim the excess with wire cutters and tuck the ends out of the way.

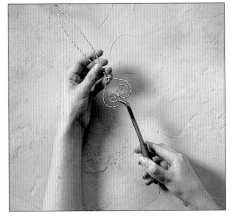

plant support

❖

This sturdy plant support is attractive enough to be on display – at least until the plant outgrows it!

MATERIALS
◆ 2mm-thick (14 gauge) twisted green gardening wire
◆ 1mm-thick (20 gauge) green gardening wire
◆ Wire cutters and ruler
◆ Bent-nose pliers

1 Cut a length of twisted wire 1²/₃yd/ 1.5m long. Bend the wire loosely in half and form a loop in the middle.

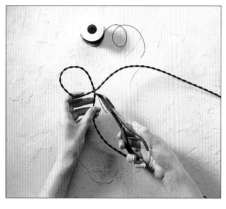

2 Bind the join three times with 1mm-thick wire to secure.

3 Cut a second length of twisted wire 3¹/₄yd/3m long. Bend loosely in half. Form two loops in the second wire 6in/15cm apart. Place the second wire near the top of the first wire and bind the two wires together.

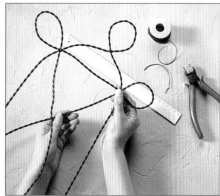

4 Bring the two ends of the long wire across each other. Bind the point where they cross. Make two more loops opposite each other 5in/13cm down the sides of the parallel base wire, binding it together with thin wire as you work.

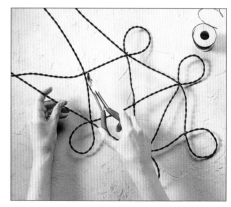

5 Continue crossing the wire, making loops and binding the wires together until there are three loops on each side. Cross the ends one last time at the center and bind to hold. Twist the excess wire around the parallel base wire.

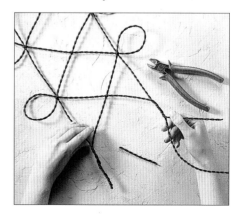

aluminum mesh basket

❖

This small mesh basket is molded over a small bowl – the mesh is folded and tucked into place and held in position with decorative wirework.

MATERIALS
◆ *Fine expanded aluminum mesh –*
9 x 10in/25 x 30cm
◆ *Bowl to use as a mold – 5 x 3¹/₂ x*
2¹/₄in/13 x 9 x 6cm deep
◆ *Scissors*
◆ *Flat-ended modeling tool*
◆ *1.25mm-thick (18 gauge), twisted gal-*
vanized wire – approximately 3m/3yd
◆ *0.75mm-thick (22 gauge), twisted gal-*
vanized wire – approximately 3yd/3m
◆ *0.3mm-thick (30 gauge), tinned*
copper wire
◆ *Round-nose pliers*
◆ *Wire cutters*
◆ *Wooden spoon*

1 Cut one piece of aluminum mesh 9 x 10in/23 x 25cm. Center the bowl on the mesh. Mold the mesh to fit the outside of the bowl. Make six small tucks at each end to ensure a neat fit. Press firmly to hold the shape.

2 Carefully and evenly cut away the excess mesh from the rim of the bowl.

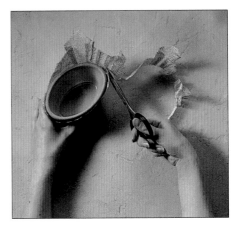

3 Remove the bowl from the mesh form.

74 ◀

4 To strengthen the basket shape, cut a length of 1.25mm (18 gauge) twisted wire to fit exactly the top of the mesh form. Hold it in place and roll the top of the mesh over the wire. Push under with the modeling tool to secure.

5 For the handle, from 0.75mm (22 gauge) wire, cut two lengths each 27½in/70cm and two lengths each 17¾in/45cm. Using pliers, form a loose spiral at each end of each wire, with the spiral facing in the same direction.

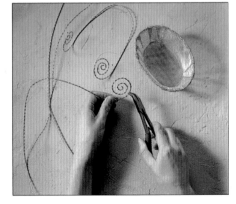

6 Twist the straight section of the long lengths together to form the handle. Turn the spirals outwards.

7 Bend back the neck of the spiral on the shorter lengths. Twist the shorter lengths one at a time onto the handle, turning the spirals inwards.

8 Position the handle over the side of the basket. Tack on the spirals through the mesh using short lengths of tinned copper wire twisted tightly together. Secure the middle and each side of the spirals as well as the point at which the handle crosses the rim. Add sufficient tacks to make the wire lie flat.

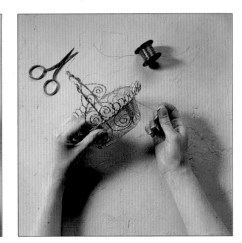

9 Secure the small spirals along the rim of the basket using tinned copper wire. Bind the spirals to the straight part of the handle, forming them into an upside-down heart.

10 Using the 0.75mm (22 gauge) twisted wire make a coil over the handle of a wooden spoon (see page 70). Flatten each loop and cut two lengths approximately 5in/13cm to fit along the basket rim at each side of the handle.

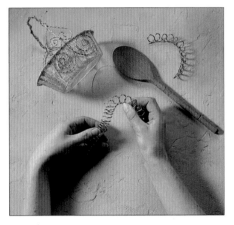

11 Bind the loop borders in place using tinned copper wire.

hand ring holder

✣

When twisting the wires together, to protect the surface of the aluminum, put a small piece of paper between the wire and the pliers.

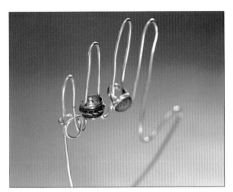

MATERIALS
- 3mm-thick (11 gauge) aluminum wire – 3¼yd/3m
- Template
- Wire cutters
- Bent-nose pliers

1 Place the end of the wire over the hand template. Leaving a 4in/10cm end of wire at the base of the palm, carefully bend the wire around the thumb and fingers.

2 Continue bending the wire around the hand and when you come to the wrist make a 90° turn.

3 Twist the 4in/10cm length of wire very tightly, three times around the remaining longer section of wire using pliers. Trim the excess from the short length only, at the back of the hand.

4 Bind the remaining longer wire length into a tight flat coil forming smooth curves with your thumb and forefinger (see picture next column).

5 Bind the coil eleven times. Trim the excess at the back of the hand.

6 Pull the coil so that it opens slightly and stands upright – the tighter coils are more difficult to manipulate.

beaded candle holder

✣

Select your favorite or most unusual colorful glass beads for this attractive candle holder.

MATERIALS
- 1.5mm-thick (16 gauge) tinned copper wire
- Tin tart form – 2¾in/7cm diameter
- Epoxy and spatula
- Faceted glass beads: shades of pink, red, purple and blue
- Bent-nose pliers
- Wire cutters
- Two hammers
- Blue tack

1 Cut eight lengths of wire 10½in/26cm long.

2 Place each wire over a solid metal base and flatten approximately 1¾in/4cm in the middle by hitting hard with the flat side of the head of a hammer.

3 Using the pliers, bend each side of the flattened center up.

4 Place each wire into the base of the form, overlaying the wires and pushing each side into opposite grooves on the

form sides. Hold the wires temporarily in place with a small piece of blue tack.

5 When all the wires are positioned mix up a quantity of the epoxy and coat the base and the wires with it. Allow it to set before removing the blue tack.

6 Using wire cutters, trim the excess wire.

7 Thread six beads onto each wire, then use the pliers to form a small loop in the top of each wire.

8 With your hands, curve the individual wires into a tulip shape.

folk art egg basket

❖

An ambitious project for those who really enjoy the decorative qualities of traditional wirework.

MATERIALS
- Twisted copper wire made with 1.5mm (16 gauge) wire
- Twisted copper wire made with 1mm (20 gauge) wire
- Flattened loops made with 1.5mm (16 gauge) copper wire
- Flattened loops made with 1mm (20 gauge) twisted copper wire
- A small roll 0.3mm-thick (30 gauge) copper binding wire
- 1mm-thick (20 gauge) copper wire
- Wire cutters
- Bent-nose pliers

1 Cut two pieces of 1.5mm (16 gauge) twisted wire one x 17in/43cm and one x 25½in/65cm.

2 Form an oval with the short length and temporarily bind the two ends together with 1mm-thick (20 gauge) wire.

3 Form the second length into a similar oval. Turn back each end at a 45° angle.

4 Using pliers form the ends into inward facing spirals.

5 Push the spirals together to form a heart and bind tightly together with 1mm (20 gauge) wire where the spirals touch and again at the base of the heart.

6 Bend the heart up so it sits at right angles to the oval (see picture next column).

7 Cut two lengths of 1mm-thick (20 gauge) wire each 12in/30cm long. Attach one end of each wire to each side of the heart by twisting the wire end twice around the twisted wire of the oval.

8 Twist the wire around the second oval 2½in/6.5cm away. Continue the wire under the base and up the opposite side, twisting around the ovals as you come to them. The oval with the heart shape will be suspended 2½in/6.5cm above the plain oval.

9 Cut two lengths of 1mm wire each 17¾in/45cm. Form one end of each into a small spiral. Attach each spiral facing inwards, at the base of the heart. Continue to weave each wire around the oval frame, finishing at the top of the opposite side. Trim any excess wire.

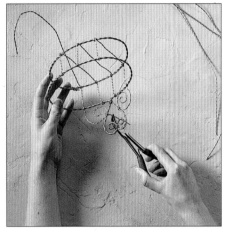

10 Cut two lengths of 1mm-thick twisted wire, each 17¾in/45cm long. Weave these wires across the oval frame, working at a right angle to the previous holding wires.

11 Cut one length of 1mm-thick twisted wire, 19¾in/50cm long. Weave this length around the walls of the basket. Twist neatly around one of the upright wires to finish.

12 Cut a 13¾in/35cm length of flattened twisted coils made from the thinner wire. Beginning at the side of the heart, bind the loops onto the top rim using fine wire.

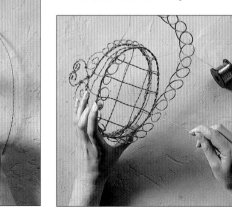

13 Cut a 17¾in/45cm length of the larger coils made with untwisted wire and bind them around the base using fine wire. As you reach the join on the base oval, remove the temporary binding and replace it with finer wire. Trim the excess coils at the point of overlap.

▶ 79

picture frame

✣

Wire is an extremely versatile material. It is readily available in many different metals and can be easily worked without the use of sophisticated techniques or specialized tools. A pair of pliers and some wire cutters are the only tools necessary to create this charming and unusually decorated frame which makes use of the pliable qualities of aluminum or tinned copper wire. The fact that it is so soft means it can easily be twisted into the looped circle.

MATERIALS
◆ *Round-nose pliers and wire cutters*
◆ *Roughly 32 blue and green glass beads with holes of more than 1mm*
◆ *Small round painted wood picture frame – 6in/15cm diameter (available from craft stores)*
◆ *1mm-thick (20 gauge) aluminum or tinned copper wire*
◆ *Strong clear glue*

1 Using the wire cutters, cut a length of the wire 2yd/2m long. Take care not to bend or twist it at this stage. Thread the beads onto the straight wire.

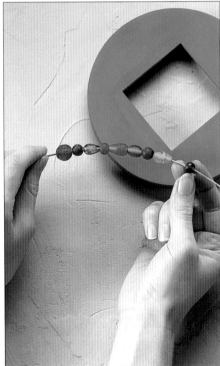

2 Keeping all the beads to the left side, start to make small loops from the right by bending the wire carefully using about 2¼in/6cm for each loop. Push a single bead into place after the first loop before making the second.

4 Fit the beaded loops around the edge of the frame, pull the wire tight as shown and twist the two ends together first with your fingers.

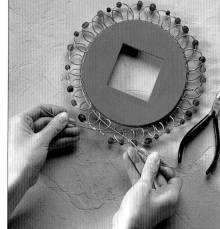

6 Turn to the back of the frame and open out the two lengths of wire. Twist the ends with the pliers to make the frame stand.

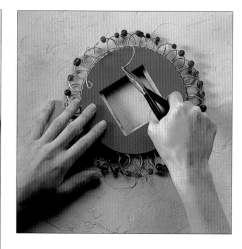

3 Continue making loops and threading the beads until you have enough to stretch around the frame. Now cut another length of wire 31½in/80cm long and thread through the loops until it makes a complete circle with an equal length of wire sticking out at each end.

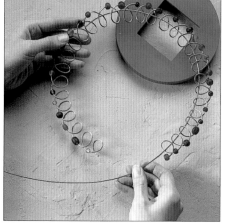

5 Twist the two ends firmly together with pliers to make a snug fit around the frame.

7 Working from the front of the frame put a dab of glue onto each end of the looped wire, place a bead onto one of the glued ends and push the other end into the bead to make an invisible join.

glass jar lantern

✣

Everyday materials like jam jars look really stunning decorated with twisted wire and with a flickering votive candle inside, suspended from the bough of a tree.

MATERIALS
◆ *1mm-thick (20 gauge) galvanized wire – one roll*
◆ *1.25mm-thick (18 gauge) galvanized wire – one roll*
◆ *Wire cutters*
◆ *Bent-nose pliers*
◆ *Jam jar*
◆ *Hand drill and vice*
◆ *Small sponge*

1 Cut two lengths of 1.25mm (18 gauge) wire, each 1⅓yd/1.25m long.

2 Cut the sponge in half and place one piece at opposite sides of the jam jar to protect the glass. Place the jam jar and sponges in the vice.

3 Place the wire around the rim of the jar and twist clockwise to hold in place.

4 Feed the ends of the wire into the chuck of the drill. Tighten to secure, then wind the drill to twist the wire to the required tension. Pull the wire to keep it taut and hold it horizontal.

5 Release the wire from the chuck, then trim the ends.

6 Turn the jar 180° in the vice, then twist the second length of wire onto the rim in the same way. Trim the wires to the same length.

7 Use the pliers to bend the wire ends into outward facing spirals, pulling the wire against your thumb to produce a smooth curve.

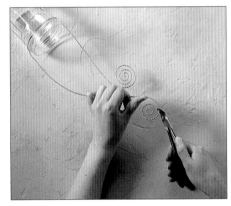

8 Bind the spirals together three times with the 1mm (20 gauge) wire. Twist at the back and trim the excess.

christmas tree decorations

❖

Twist a second color wire into the structure of the scrolls and complement the color scheme with an attractive glass bead.

MATERIALS
◆ *1.25mm-thick (18 gauge) galvanized wire – one roll*
◆ *0.5mm-thick (26 gauge) pink anodized aluminum wire – a small reel*
◆ *Wire cutters*
◆ *Bent-nose pliers*
◆ *Glass beads – two small opaque, one red heart, two pink cut-glass*
◆ *Small scissors*

1 Twist together the two lengths of wire following the instructions on page 69.

2 Using wire cutters, cut four lengths of twisted wire each 8¾in/22cm.

3 Form one end of each length into a large loose spiral. Make a curve in the central section, then form a tight spiral at the other end. Make four.

4 Cut one length of pink wire 8¾in/ 22cm. Thread a small opaque bead half way along. Bend the wire in two around the bead, then thread the remaining beads onto both wires.

5 Put the four scrolls together, with the bend facing outwards. Place the beaded wire in the center of the large scroll. Tightly bind the top join approximately eight times with pink wire.

6 Twist the ends together to secure. Bind the base in the same manner.

7 Open out the shape, ensuring that the scrolls are evenly spaced.

cat face bird scarer

❖

On a light spring or summer's day, these decorative cats will be sure to scare away the birds.

MATERIALS

◆ 0.15mm-thick copper foil – 12in/ 30cm square

◆ 2mm-thick (14 gauge) copper wire – one roll
◆ Tracing paper, pencil and glue
◆ Card stock
◆ Dry ballpoint pen and small coin
◆ Small-pointed scissors
◆ Tracing wheel
◆ Old phone book
◆ Epoxy and spatula
◆ Transparent tape
◆ Two glass marbles
◆ Bent-nose pliers
◆ Bamboo cane

1 To make a template, trace or photo-copy the pattern provided. Stick the copy to card stock and cut out. Tape the template to the copper foil.

2 Draw the outline with a ballpoint pen, pressing lightly to transfer the shape onto the metal.

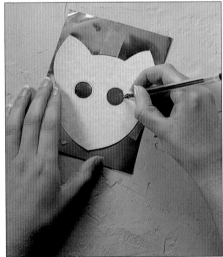

3 Cut out the face and remove the circles marked for the eyes. Using the points of the scissors, snip all around the edges of the eyes, to make sure that the marbles will fit neatly.

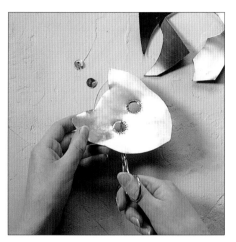

4 Place the face on the phone book. With the tracing wheel, outline the face, circle the eyes and outline the ears. Use the ballpoint pen to draw in the nose, mouth and the effect of fur in the ears and over the top of the face. Press firmly to make sure the design is clearly marked.

5 Mark the whiskers with the tracing wheel.

6 Turn over to the right side of the face. Mix up the epoxy and apply all around the perimeter of the eyes. Place each marble in the eye, over the glue and allow to dry. Support the underside of the face so that the marbles do not come out.

7 Cut a 12in/30cm length of copper wire. Use the pliers to make a double loop at one end, ensuring that the two loops are firmly closed together.

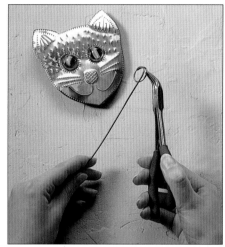

▶ 85

8 Make a mix of epoxy and slide the base of the face between the loops. Fill the space inside the loop with glue making sure that both the wire and metal are covered. Stick wire in bamboo cane.

metal foil flowers

❖

Use all three metals – copper, aluminum and brass – to make these delicate flowers.

MATERIALS
- 0.1mm brass foil or shim – one roll
- 0.1mm-thick scraps of copper and aluminum foil – 1 ¼ x 4in/3 x 10cm
- 1mm- and 1.5mm-thick (20 and 16 gauge) copper wire – approximately 12in/30cm per flower
- Tracing paper and pencil
- Thin card stock and glue
- Dry ballpoint pen
- Transparent tape
- Old phone book
- Tracing wheel
- Small-pointed scissors
- Medium-size scissors
- Awl
- Epoxy and spatula
- Pliers

1 To make a template, trace or photo-copy the pattern provided. Stick the copy to card stock and cut out. Tape the template to the brass foil.

2 Draw the outline with a ballpoint pen, pressing lightly to transfer the image.

3 Cut out the shape using small scissors. Pierce the center with the awl, insert the point of the scissors and cut out the circle.

4 Place the flower on the phone book. Use the tracing wheel to mark the lines between the petals.

5 Turn the flower over and mark the longer lines in the center of the petals and around the edge of the flower. This method creates a three-dimensional effect.

6 To make stamens, cut one length each of aluminum, copper and brass foil 1¼ x 4in/3 x 10cm.

7 Snip closely along one side – the snipped edge will curl automatically giving the frilly appearance of a stamen.

8 Cut a 12in/30cm length of 1.5mm (16 gauge) wire and make a small loop at one end using pliers.

9 Wind the frilly brass foil tightly around the wire, then add the copper and finally the aluminum.

10 Pinch the frilly edge of foil onto the wire stem using pliers.

11 Thread through the flower center, push firmly against the petals.

12 Make a mix of glue. Use the spatula to apply glue around the underside of the petals where they meet the stem. Allow to dry.

13 Wind a 12in/30cm length of 1mm-thick (20 gauge) copper wire tightly around the stem. Allow the glue to nearly dry.

14 Continue up the stem and wind around the base of the flower head making sure that the untidy join is neatly covered. Cut off the excess wire.

brass butterfly

✤

These three-dimensional shapes are simple to make. Their bodies are molded around a wooden spoon handle and their antennae are springy coils of foil.

MATERIALS

◆ *0.1mm-thick brass foil or shim – one roll*
◆ *Tracing paper and pencil*
◆ *Thin card stock and epoxy*
◆ *Transparent tape*
◆ *Dry ballpoint pen and a small coin*
◆ *Small-pointed scissors*
◆ *Old phone book*
◆ *Two sizes of tracing wheel*
◆ *Wooden spoon and knitting needle*
◆ *Brass picture wire*

1 To make a template, trace or photo-copy one of the patterns provided. Stick the copy to the card stock and cut out. Tape the template to the brass foil and draw around the shape pressing lightly with a ballpoint pen.

2 Remove the template. Using small-pointed scissors cut out the butterfly. Be careful when cutting the antennae. Cut between each pair of wings.

3 Place the butterfly on an old phone book. Outline the body and wings with a large tracing wheel. Mark a circle on each wing by drawing around a coin with a dry ballpoint pen.

4 Use the smaller tracing wheel to make stars in the circles and lines across the body. Use the larger wheel along each antennae and make three lines where each wing joins the body.

5 Turn the butterfly to the right side. Bend the wings into position. Curl the body section around the handle of a wooden spoon.

6 To make the antennae, roll each tightly around a knitting needle as shown in the picture below. Remove the needle and loosen the coil.

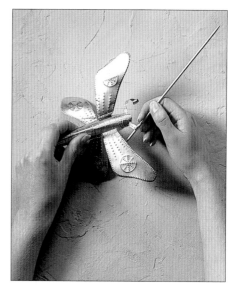

7 Use epoxy to secure a small brass wire hook to the back of the body. This allows the butterfly to be hung.

house candle shade

✤

Soften lighting with these unusual candle holders, inspired by traditional Mexican crafts. Made in the form of a simple house, these shades look stunning when the light shines through the windows and the punched holes.

MATERIALS

- ◆ *0.1mm-thick aluminum foil*
- ◆ *Tracing paper, glue*
- ◆ *Dry ballpoint pen*
- ◆ *Ruler and pencil*
- ◆ *Craft knife and thin card stock*

- ◆ *Two tracing wheels – one with closely spaced and one with widely spaced wheels*
- ◆ *Old phone book*
- ◆ *Small-pointed scissors*
- ◆ *Transparent tape*

1 To make a template, trace or photocopy the pattern provided. Stick the copy to card stock and cut out. Tape the template to the aluminum foil. Draw the outlines of the house, windows and door with a ballpoint pen, pressing lightly to transfer the shape.

2 Use the ruler and pen to draw lightly over the lines marked on the template – these will appear as indented lines on the metal.

3 Remove the template and cut carefully around the shape. To cut the windows, first make a cut in each corner with a craft knife, then push the scissors through.

4 Place the foil right side down on the phone book. Draw lines around the windows with the small tracing wheel, pressing firmly to transfer the design.

5 Using the larger tracing wheel and a ruler, redraw the lightly drawn guide lines. Press very hard so that the points on the wheel pierce through the metal. Use a ruler for drawing the straight lines.

6 With the help of a ruler, bend the roof at a 45° angle. Bend the chimneys upright, then bend each side at right angles to the house front.

crown hook rack

✛

This hook rack, with its regal theme, can be adapted to suit any room of the house.

MATERIALS

◆ 0.1mm-thick copper foil
◆ 0.3mm-thick (30 gauge) reel of copper wire
◆ 1mm-thick (20 gauge) twisted copper wire – approximately 3yd/3m
◆ 1.5mm-thick (16 gauge) copper wire – one reel
◆ Tracing paper and pencil
◆ Thin card stock and glue
◆ Transparent tape
◆ Old phone book
◆ Small piece of wood
◆ Small-pointed scissors
◆ Dry ballpoint pen
◆ Tracing wheel
◆ Bent-nose pliers
◆ Long-nose pliers
◆ Awl
◆ Wire cutters

1 To make a template, trace or photo-copy the pattern provided. Stick the copy to card stock and cut out.

2 Tape the template to the copper foil. Draw around the outline with a dry ball-point pen pressing lightly to transfer the image.

3 Carefully cut out the shape using small pointed scissors. Snip off the sharp corners.

4 Place the crown on the directory. Outline the crown using the tracing wheel. Draw two parallel lines across the lower part of the design. Divide the section between the lines into three and mark the design in each section. Add a scroll pattern to the top half of the design.

5 To make the loop decoration, cut a length of 1mm-thick (20 gauge) twisted copper wire 15¾in/40cm. At one end, fold 1in/2cm up at a right angle. Bend the wire into a rectangular shape to correspond with the section at the base of the crown below the parallel line decoration. Bring it around to where it meets. Make another 90° turn of 1¼in/3cm to match the beginning.

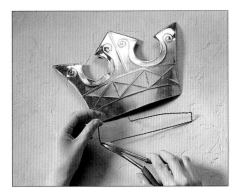

6 Cut and manipulate a row of flattened loops so that they fit into the wire shape made at step 4. Use the fine wire to bind the loops in place.

7 Cut 4in/10cm lengths of the twisted wire and use the pliers to bend one end to make them into hooks.

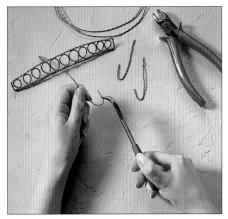

8 Place the crown right side up, over the piece of wood. Use the awl to pierce four holes along the base line of the crown – one in the middle of each section and one larger one at the join between the first and second sections (see picture next column).

9 Push the two ends of the loop decoration through the larger hole. Bend the top 1in/2cm of each hook over at right angles and push these through the designated holes.

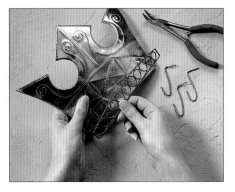

10 Turn the crown over. Use the long-nose pliers to bend and flatten any protruding wire ends.

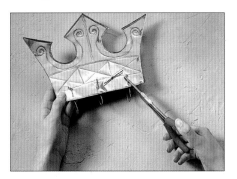

brass gloved hand clasp

❖

These Victorian-style little gloved hands ingeniously disguise a wooden peg clasp. The glowing color of brass is similar in appearance to gold and polishes beautifully. Use them to hold all types of items from stamps to ribbons.

MATERIALS

- ◆ 0.1mm-thick brass foil or shim – one roll
- ◆ Tracing paper and pencil
- ◆ Thin card stock and glue
- ◆ Transparent tape

- ◆ Small-pointed scissors
- ◆ Tracing wheel
- ◆ Dry ballpoint pen.
- ◆ Old phone book
- ◆ Quick-setting epoxy and spatula
- ◆ Wooden clothes peg

1 To make a template, trace or photo-copy the pattern provided. Stick the copy to card and cut out. Tape the template to the metal foil.

2 Draw around it with a dry ballpoint pen to transfer the shape.

3 Cut out carefully, being careful around the intricate areas between the fingers.

4 Place the glove right side down on the phone book and decorate the surface with the tracing wheel, pressing firmly. The design will appear as a raised pattern on the right side. Trace a line all around the edge of the glove and decorate the cuff.

5 With the pen, make dots where the fingers join the hand and along the band around the wrist. Mark the spirals and the star on the back of the hand and the pattern on the cuff.

6 Mix a small quantity of epoxy. Use the spatula to apply it in a straight line along the wrong side of the hand to corre-spond with the length of the peg.

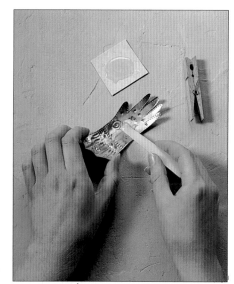

▶ 95

7 Stick the peg to this glued area, mak-ing sure the lever end matches the cuff. Put a weight onto the peg and leave the glue to set.

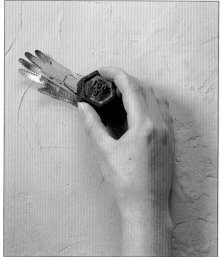

bird greeting card

✥

These embossed greeting cards are simple to decorate using a tracing wheel and punched stars.

MATERIALS
◆ 0.1mm-thick copper foil
◆ Tracing paper and pencil
◆ Thin card stock and glue
◆ Transparent tape
◆ Double-sided tape
◆ Old phone book
◆ Dry ballpoint pen
◆ Brown card stock – 6¼ x 8½in/ 16 x 22cm
◆ Tracing wheel
◆ Blue handmade paper 6¼ x 3½in/ 16 x 9cm
◆ Small-pointed scissors
◆ Pinking shears
◆ Star punch and hammer
◆ Small piece of wood

1 To make a template, trace or photocopy the pattern provided. Stick the copy to card and cut out. Tape the template to the copper. Draw the outline with a ballpoint pen pressing lightly to transfer the design.

2 Remove the template. Cut out the shape.

3 Place the shape right side down on an old directory. Outline the shape, pressing firmly with the tracing wheel. "Draw" two parallel lines at the base of the neck, then four lines to separate the tail from the body (see picture next column).

4 With the tracing wheel, draw two lines at each side of the wing.

5 Transfer the bird to the wood surface. Using a hammer, punch five stars along the center of the wing, one for the eye and five along the tip of the tail.

6 Fold the brown card stock in half so that it stands with the opening at the base.

7 Trim the edge of the blue paper with pinking shears. Apply two strips of double-sided tape to one side.

8 Center the blue rectangle, then stick in place on the brown card stock.

9 Center the bird on the paper and stick in place using the double-sided tape.

10 Press lightly to ensure the bird is secure.

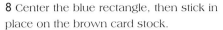

cheese larder

❖

A combination of wire- and metalwork techniques has been used to create this useful and decorative cheese larder.

MATERIALS

◆ 0.1mm-thick brass foil – one roll
◆ 0.3mm-thick (30 gauge) brass wire – one reel
◆ Woven brass gauze
◆ Braided brass picture wire – 1yd/1m
◆ Tracing paper and pencil
◆ Thin card stock and glue
◆ Dry ballpoint pen and coin
◆ Transparent tape

◆ Old phone book
◆ Small hole punch
◆ Tracing wheel
◆ Brass tacks and hammer
◆ Small-scale wooden cupboard with the front panel cut away

1 To make a template, trace or photocopy the pattern provided. Stick the copy to card stock and cut out.

2 Tape the template to the brass foil and draw around the shape pressing lightly with a ballpoint pen.

3 Remove the templates and place the foil onto the phone book. Mark the leaf veins and the petals with the tracing wheel.

4 Draw around the coin to make the flower center. Then make five flowers, six leaves and one flowerpot.

5 With the tracing wheel, draw the pot outline. Draw three circles in the top section and decorate them with tracing wheel stars. Make dots between these with the point of the ballpoint pen.

6 Add a lattice-work design to the lower section of the pot.

7 Cut carefully around all the shapes. For safety, cut off the sharp corners of the pot.

8 Using the hole punch, make holes in each end of the leaves, on the tip of alternate flower petals, then three evenly-spaced holes up each side of the pot.

9 Cut a piece of gauze 1¼in/3cm larger all around than the panel in the cupboard door. With a pencil, draw the shape of the panel in the center of the gauze.

10 Center the pot ¾in/2cm above the drawn baseline. Secure by tying the fine brass wire through the punched holes and through the gauze. Twist to secure tightly on the wrong side (see picture next column).

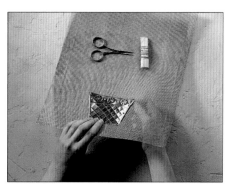

11 Cut five braded brass lengths: one x 7in/18cm, two x 5½in/14cm and two x 3¼in/8cm. Slot each wire behind the pot and tie onto the gauze using fine wire. Secure as before.

12 Place one flower on each stem and tie in place.

13 Add two leaves to each of the three central stems.

14 Check that all the ties are secure on the back of the gauze, then trim the excess.

15 Position the gauze over the space on the inside of the cupboard door, ensuring the design is facing in the correct direction. Push a line of brass tacks into the frame all around the gauze and hammer in place.

▶ 99

christmas reindeer

❖

This magical herd of reindeer make a stunning and unusual Christmas decoration.

MATERIALS
◆ *0.1mm-thick aluminium foil –*
6in/15cm square for each reindeer
◆ *Tracing paper and pencil*
◆ *Thin card stock and glue*
◆ *Dry ballpoint pen*
◆ *Transparent tape*
◆ *Small-pointed scissors*
◆ *Old phone book*
◆ *Bent-nose pliers*

1 To make a template, trace or photo-copy the pattern provided. Stick the copy to card stock and cut out.

2 Tape the templates onto the aluminum foil. Draw around each outline.

3 Remove the templates. Carefully cut out each shape using small-pointed scissors. Take special care with the antlers.

4 Place the shapes on an old phone book. Mark the body pattern by pressing with a dry ballpoint pen. Mark short lines along the back and then at right angles down the legs. Mark the eye, mouth, antlers and neck.

5 Cut a ⅛in/0.5cm slit at each side of the base of the neck, ⅛in/0.5cm up from the base. Turn the cut sections in and press flat.

6 Make a slit in the front of the reindeer body large enough to fit the base of the neck through. Push the neck through the slit.

7 To secure the head firmly to the body, turn the body to the wrong side and use the pliers to open out the folded-in sections.

8 Bend the tab at the front of the body down, then bend the body over to enable the reindeer to stand.

foil wreath

❖

Silver aluminum is the perfect metal with which to create the subtly decorated willow leaves which make up this wintry wreath.

MATERIALS

◆ 0.1mm-thick aluminum foil – one roll
◆ Tracing paper, thin card stock and glue
◆ 1mm-thick (20 gauge) galvanized wire – one roll
◆ Twisted galvanized wire made from 1.5mm (16 gauge) wire – 8½in/22cm
◆ 0.3mm-thick (30 gauge) tinned copper binding wire – one reel
◆ Tracing wheel and awl
◆ Small-pointed scissors
◆ Dry ballpoint pen and pencil
◆ Old phone book
◆ Small block of wood
◆ Transparent tape

1 Using twisted wire, form a circle with a 7in/18cm diameter. Bind the join with the 1mm wire.

2 To make a template, trace or photocopy the pattern provided. Stick the copy to card stock and cut out. Tape the templates to the metal foil and draw around each using a ballpoint pen. Draw 50 in total. Remove the templates.

3 Place the foil on the phone book. Use the tracing wheel to mark the leaf veins. One leaf has an outline and a central vein. The other has veins radiating from the central vein.

4 Carefully cut out the leaves. Clip off any sharp points.

5 Place each leaf on the wood and push the tip of the awl through the base of each leaf to make a very small hole.

6 Thread fine wire through the hole and bind it tightly onto the twisted wire circle. Thread the leaf shapes alternately and space evenly to complete the circle.

7 Add a second layer of leaves overlapping the first, threading each onto the circle as before.

▶ 103

8 Manipulate the leaves with your finger, bending, twisting and curling them slightly to give a more natural appearance.

plant name marker

❖

These copper plant tags are suitable as a first project for a beginner.

MATERIALS

- ◆ 0.1mm-thick copper foil
- ◆ Tracing paper and pencil
- ◆ Thin card stock and glue
- ◆ Dry ballpoint pen
- ◆ Two different-sized tracing wheels
- ◆ Star punch and hammer
- ◆ Small-pointed scissors
- ◆ Transparent tape
- ◆ Old phone book
- ◆ Small block of wood

1 To make a template, trace or photocopy the pattern provided. Stick the copy to card stock and cut out. Tape the template to copper foil and draw around it with the ballpoint pen to make an indent. Cut out each shape.

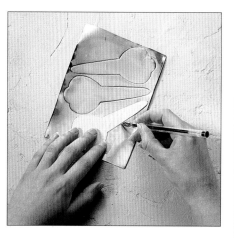

2 Place each shape on an old phone book. Draw around the edge with the small tracing wheel, pressing firmly to create the indented dotted line. The pattern will appear as a raised design on the right side of the key.

3 In the same way, roll the larger tracing wheel along the middle of the "stem" to produce a similar pattern.

4 Place the plant marker on a piece of wood. Position the star punch at the top, then at the base of the central section. Hit with the hammer to transfer the design.

5 To finish, using the phone book for a surface, write the name of the plant in the central section with a dry ballpoint pen.

t e m p l a t e s

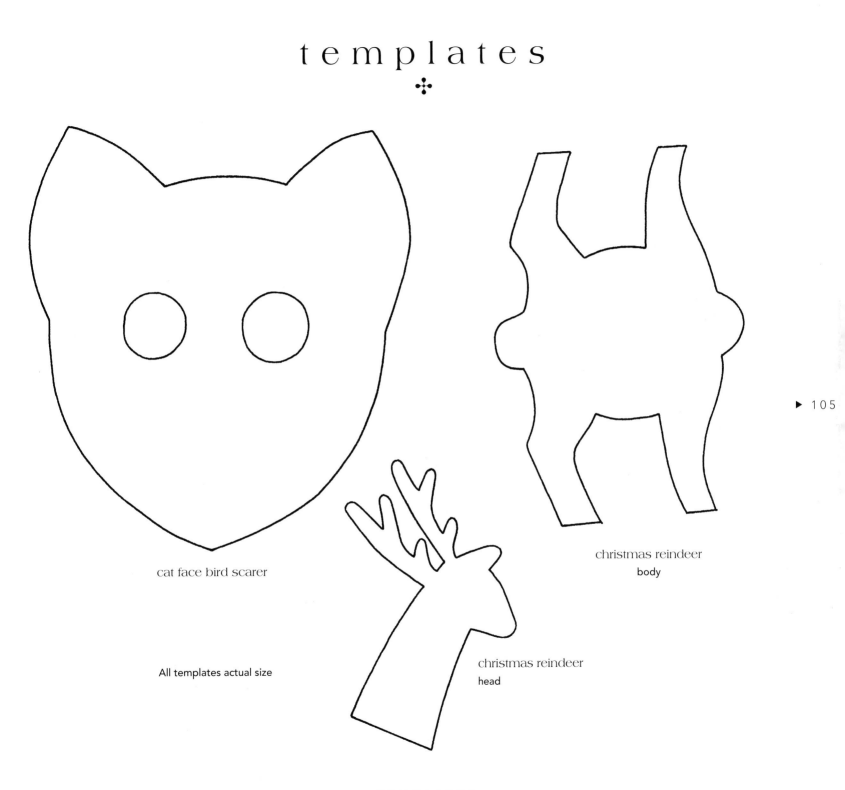

cat face bird scarer

All templates actual size

christmas reindeer
head

christmas reindeer
body

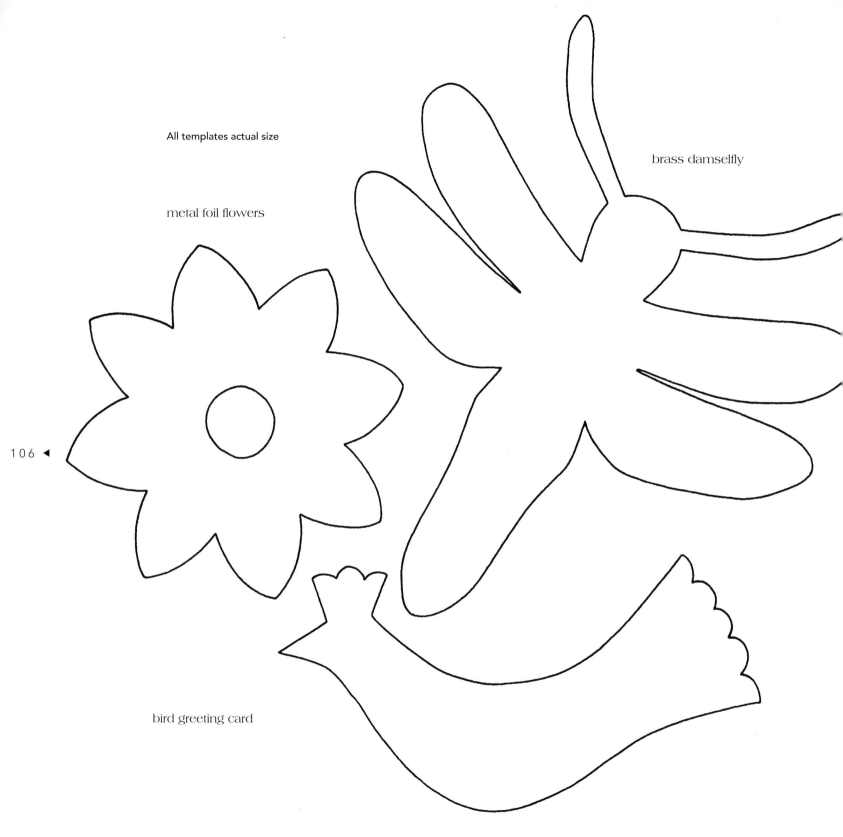

All templates actual size

brass damselfly

metal foil flowers

bird greeting card

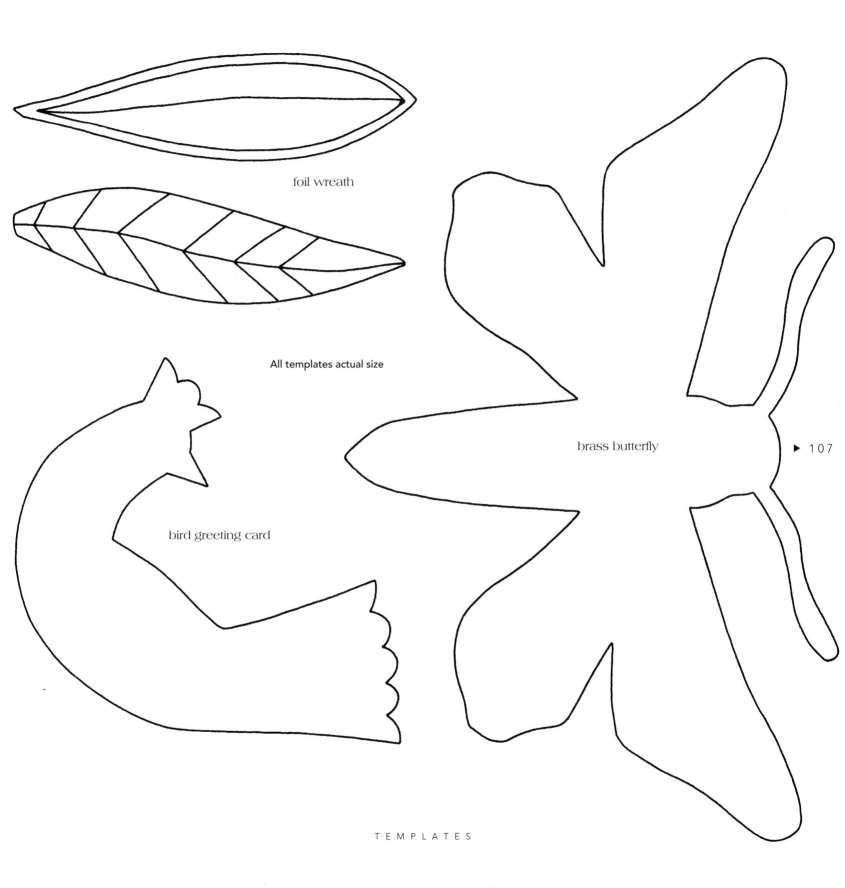

foil wreath

All templates actual size

bird greeting card

brass butterfly

▶ 107

TEMPLATES

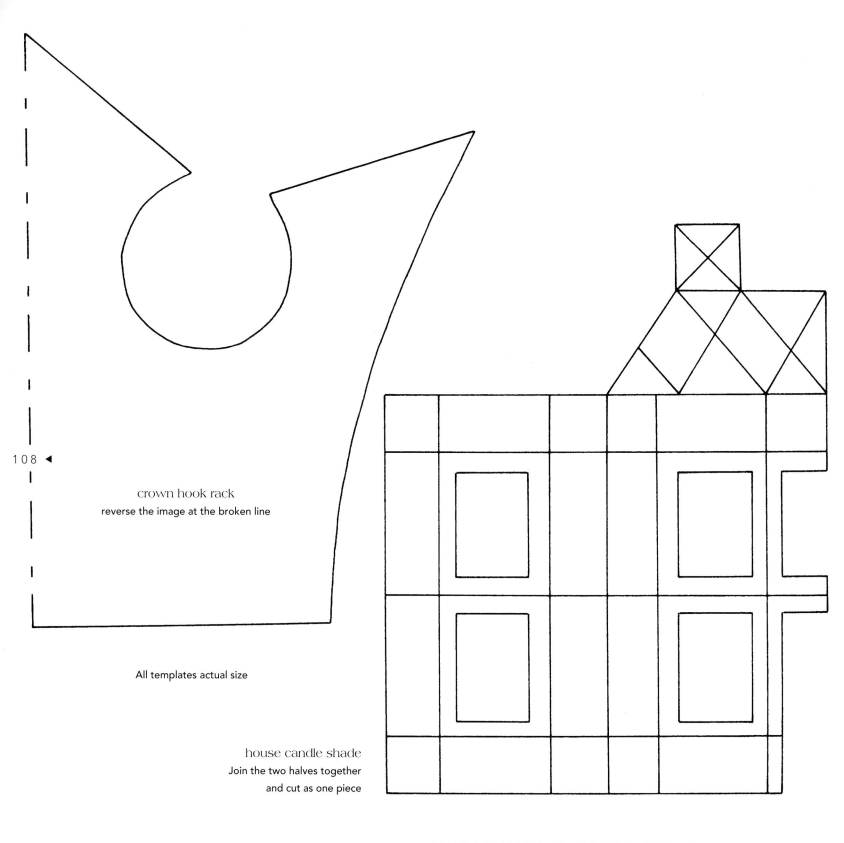

crown hook rack
reverse the image at the broken line

All templates actual size

house candle shade
Join the two halves together
and cut as one piece

All templates
actual size

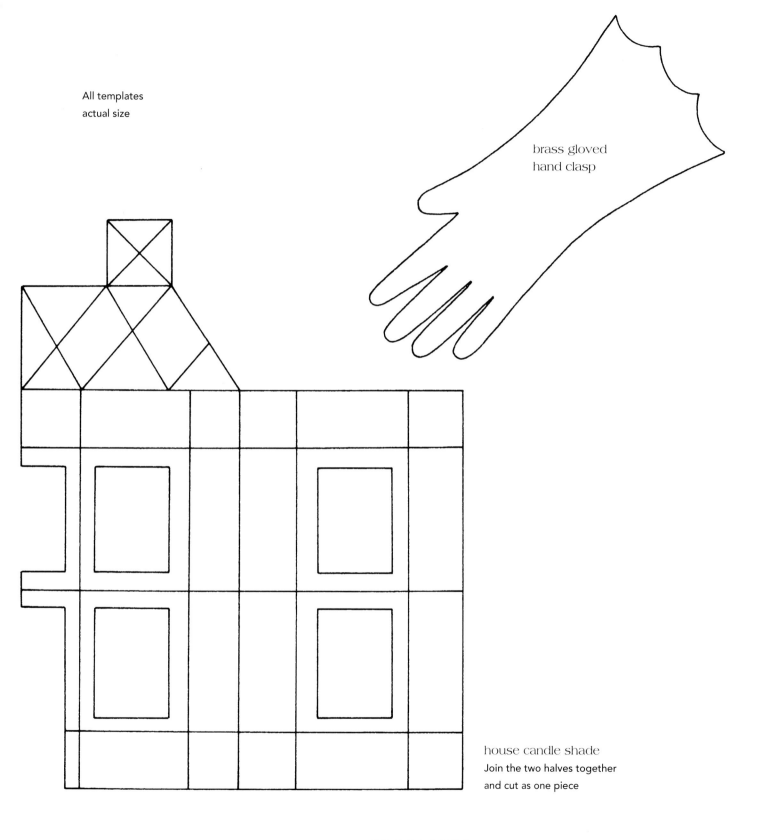

brass gloved
hand clasp

house candle shade
Join the two halves together
and cut as one piece

TEMPLATES

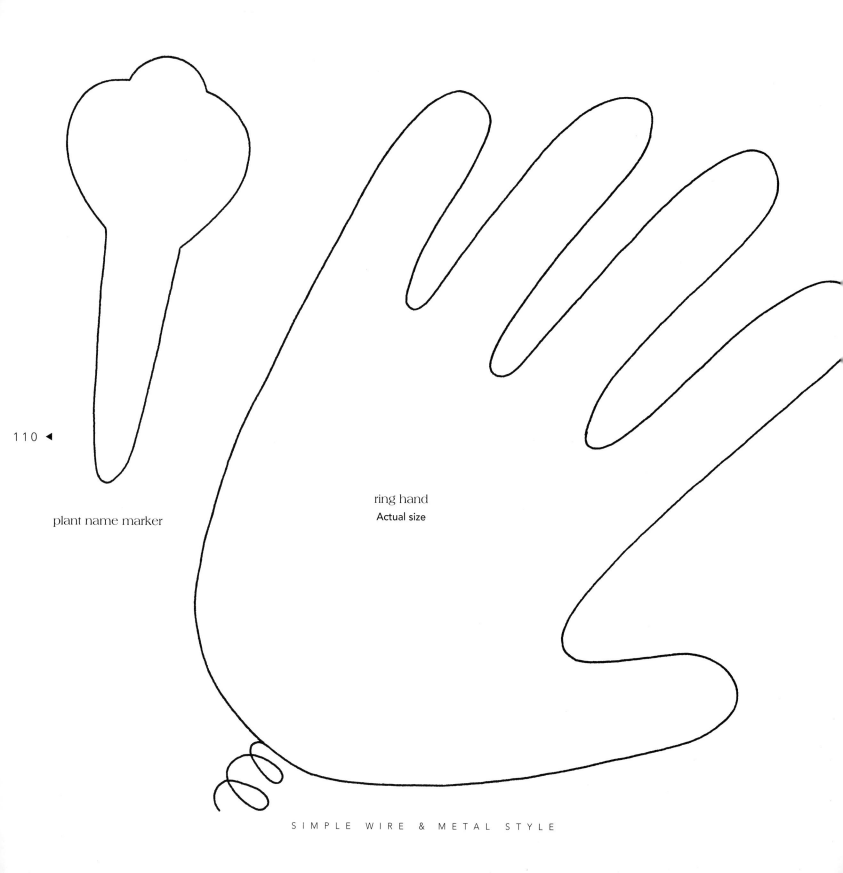

plant name marker

ring hand
Actual size

All templates
actual size

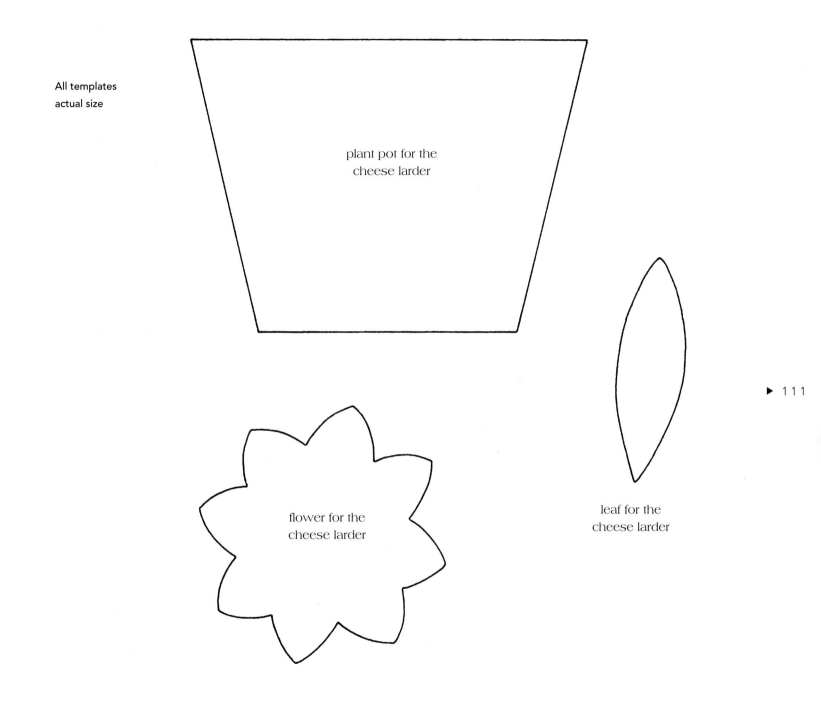

plant pot for the
cheese larder

flower for the
cheese larder

leaf for the
cheese larder

▶ 111

index

✤